Soul
(Wholeness for the Body, Soul, and Mind)

A Simple Prayer and Meditation Project

Traci A. Vanderbush

This book and other works by Traci Vanderbush are
available at tracivanderbush.wix.com/vanderbush or at
Amazon.com.

Introduction

Welcome to a simple journey in what I refer to as "soul reformation." Some may think the term sounds mystical or strange, but our bodies and souls were created by a very creative Creator, and He delights in restoration and repair. In fact, He is known for making all things new.

In this life on earth, we encounter many challenges. Every person, at some point in their life, will find themselves in the midst of a battle. For some, there are multiple battles on many levels. It is my desire to bring hope and relief to those who are facing trauma. I am not a doctor or a psychologist, but I am a human who's had my own share of trauma, and I've experienced relief when I center myself on the reality of my soul being enveloped in the love of God. Whether mild or severe, trauma impacts us, but I believe that with God, we have hope for healing, whether instantaneous or gradual.

Life on earth is a beautiful moment, a quickly passing moment in which we strive to find and fulfill our purpose and destiny. Sadly, the world is filled with people who do not know their value and purpose, but how wonderful it is that we get to be a light in their darkness. Even in our own darkness, the light still shines out. I believe it is that light, the light of Jesus Christ that draws us into the fullness of what we were created for.

You are literally a dream of God. He thought of you long before you were formed. This statement could launch me into doing a theological study in this book, listing scriptures and other evidence of this thought, but in doing so, I would be diverting from the purpose of this project. I encourage you to do your own study and searching.

Your soul was already thriving in God before He fashioned you with His hands and infused you with His breath. As we walk through this journey of life, we must remember that what we know now is temporal. Though it be temporal, we are fully eternal, and what we know now is just the tip of the iceberg.

No matter how wonderful or how horrible your life may be thus far, I pray that you would know there are many good days ahead for you. Goodness and mercy follow you all the days of your life, and your Father goes before you. Life's disappointments may try to convince you otherwise, but the negatives, tragedies, and hardships do not have the power to dictate what the rest of your life will look like. After all, anything is possible with God. All things are possible. To put it another way, nothing is impossible. Do not limit yourself based on the shortcomings and failures you have experienced. Always believe and keep believing.

There's a line in a song that has always moved me and pressed me forward when life has thrown challenges my way. The song is from Disney's Cinderella movie. "A Dream is a Wish Your Heart Makes," carries a sentiment that seems impossible, but can you imagine this to be true:

No matter how your heart is grieving
If you keep on believing
The dream that you wish will come true.

How can that be possible? Many, including myself, have said, "That's not possible. My dream is dead. It's gone and nothing can change that." Yes, some things we dreamed about are no longer an option for us, yet God has a beautifully incredible way of making that dream still come true, perhaps in another way or another form. Perhaps the dream will be revived outside of the box of time that we've locked ourselves into.

Some things cannot be changed without a time machine or a "do-over," yet I believe God is capable of and desires to make all things new. He is not a dream-killer, but a dream-giver. The dream-giver is often blamed for the bad things that happen throughout life, but I do not believe He authors those things. We live in a world where our hearts and lives are at the mercy of one another, so we suffer due to the choices of others and the choices we make. I've witnessed the intervention of God many times, yet there are situations in which it seemed He did not. I don't have answers for that, but I still believe He weeps with us and He will absolutely make something that's senseless and ugly into something beautiful. I believe darkness will ultimately backfire on itself. Tragedy will never win.

Some of our dreams won't be seen for us until we fully enter His realm, but we are still empowered to make dreams come true on this earth, to leave a legacy that will launch others into their dreams come true. Your perseverance matters. Your life matters. Though you may feel minute or hidden, what you do matters. Your thoughts and words matter to someone. Your acts of kindness are life to another soul. Your voice carries the power to create a new reality for someone in need. Your actions are loaded with the potential to influence and heal broken hearts. Souls can be repaired at your hands.

Why "soul reformation?" What does that mean?

I do not claim to have all the answers for your healing, yet from my own experience, I've found what is in this book to be helpful. Each person's experience is different. For me, soul repair or reformation is the active, conscious placing of your soul into the hands of your Creator, engaging all of your senses toward Him. It requires focusing your body, mind and soul on His goodness. It's about intimacy; spending time saturated in the presence of Him.

In this life, your soul will be wounded at times, but there is more goodness available for you that we often forfeit due to forgetfulness. It seems the negative experiences often overshadow the good ones. In actively engaging our senses toward the Father, we give room to focus on and be grateful for the nourishment that our soul needs. There is something wonderful about taking a moment to let Him feed your soul. In doing so, we can help others.

There is scientific evidence that what is going on inside of us (in our minds and hearts) affects our bodies and those around us. There are plenty of expert books and writings on this subject, so I won't attempt to explain. You have access to this information via the internet and your local library. I encourage you to find out more about how the way you think affects your body. This is an enlightening topic to research. It's no wonder why the scriptures of old teach us to think on things that are good, lovely, and right.

In order to care for our bodies, we must not only focus on diet and exercise, but also our souls and minds. We can exercise and eat healthy foods, but our minds will make us sick if our soul is not well. The mind is powerful. The media knows this well. They also know how easy it is for us to grasp onto bad news. They know the key words that grab our attention: danger, dangerous, shocking, revealing, biggest, worst, avoid, must know, catastrophic, record-breaking, unprecedented, etc. The list goes on and on. I have often wondered why we more easily and rapidly spread bad news than good news. Our fascination with what is wrong is the very poison we use against ourselves, making us blind and deaf to all that is right.

What words would capture our attention for the good news? What would happen in the world if we were quick to spread word of every good thing that was happening? I have no doubt that goodness outweighs the bad. To elevate evil above good would be to deny God. To elevate the amount of sin above the amount of righteousness would be to deny the power of Christ and all that He accomplished. Our minds were created to be aware of the presence and power of God and Him in us, to create with Him and accomplish great works.

Why did I write this?

Like most every person who is reading this, I have experienced trauma, both physical and emotional. There was a time when I felt I might be destroyed by emotional pain. Have you been there? I walked through that valley and discovered that light exists even in the darkness. Thankfully, I didn't remain in the valley. When we are in that place, it's difficult to feel hope, but I promise you, there is always hope. It's alive and well. The dark moments, often referred to as "the dark night of the soul," try to convince us that things can never be any better than they already are. It's a veil, a shroud to block our vision to what is possible.

Apart from the season of emotional pain that I referred to, I experienced a traumatic car accident in 2015 that resulted in physical pain that still surfaces at times. Just recently, something really amazing happened, and that amazing moment is what inspired me to create this prayer and meditation project for you. I hope that others will benefit from my experience. Here is what happened.

The Car Accident

My husband and I were driving past the scene of the accident and I began pointing out where my car had come to a stop and where the other vehicle rolled over. In passing the scene and remembering that moment when I stepped out of the car, seeing with tunnel vision, ears ringing, the smell of gun powder in my nose, my heartbeat pounding as I tried to stand without passing out...just the memory of it all caused my body to hurt.

Later that day, I was overcome by pain in the very places where those old injuries were. My forearm and chest throbbed. My whole body felt as if I'd been beaten with a 2x4. I wondered, "What in the world is going on? This is ridiculous!" I was shocked by the ability of a memory to inflict me with pain. I've heard about muscle memory and cell memory, but I failed to realize its power until that point. I spent the evening praying and pondering. I decided that if a traumatic, negative memory had the power to make me feel awful, surely good memories and happy moments contained even more power to affect me.

I asked the Holy Spirit to teach me more about this. A prayer came to mind as I laid my hands on my upper chest. I began speaking the words to my body as they flowed through my mind.

Later that night, laughter kept hitting me unexpectedly. Do you remember being a child and having a moment when you couldn't stop laughing, even at the most inappropriate time? Do you recall thinking that everything was funny? That's exactly what happened to me that night. Lying in bed, I closed my eyes, expecting to fall asleep. As my mind began the process of entering sleep mode, funny pictures began flashing through my mind. A couple of images were of stuffed animals that I owned as a child. In this dream zone, I felt things I had long forgotten. Happy, carefree memories filled my mind. My senses were fully alive and awakened! I smelled things that brought warm, joyful thoughts. Throughout the night, I woke myself up with audible giggling. The next morning, I was without pain.

For the next two days, this continued. Occasionally, I still struggle with moments of those negative things arising, but I've found this prayer and meditation to be very helpful in centering myself back on Christ. In Him, there is no lack.

You may think, "Well, my childhood was awful, so this is impossible." Though I had a good, loving home, I also experienced sexual abuse at the hands of a neighbor, so I do understand that not everyone has a perfectly blissful childhood. I know that many of you may have grown up in abusive homes, so I don't want to make light of those situations. I do believe that no matter how dark it may have been, there must have been some moments of joy for you. Was it a piece of candy? A special doll or toy? Was it a friend? What brought you comfort and safety? Whatever it was that brought you a smile or glimmer of hope still exists within you. If you cannot recall any moments of joy, I pray they will come to the surface and bring you peace.

What was the prayer that I prayed?

In the following pages, immerse yourself in the words that were impressed in my spirit. The words are combined with pictures I have taken in various places where I felt drawn to stop and listen. Have you ever been someplace that drew tears to your eyes? Have you ever stood in a moment that made you aware of the Father? The photographs I've included are places where I could feel the Father drawing me in; and I could feel the earth speaking.

Perhaps certain photos will draw you in. I pray that certain words and pictures will capture you and move you. Pay attention when that happens. I encourage you to not just read this one time, but to make it a continual practice until you experience a drastic change for your soul and body.

The Holy Spirit is a good teacher for the body, and the body is subject to the Holy Spirit. May you experience wholeness and peace in the following pages.

Be blessed.

~Traci

First, a word about meditation...

Meditate:
Intransitive verb
1. to engage in contemplation or reflection
2. to engage in mental exercise for the purpose of reaching a heightened level of spiritual awareness

Transitive verb
1. to focus one's thoughts on, reflect or ponder over
2. to plan or project in the mind

(Merriam-Webster)

Scriptures about meditation:

Genesis 24:63 Isaac went out to meditate in the field toward evening...

Joshua 1:8 This book of the law shall not depart from your mouth, but you shall meditate on it day and night...

Psalm 1:2 But his delight is in the law of the Lord, and in His law he meditates day and night.

Psalm 4:4 Tremble and do not sin; Meditate in your heart upon your bed and be still.

Psalm 27:4 One thing I have asked from the Lord, that I shall seek: that I may dwell in the house of the Lord all the days of my life, to behold the beauty of the Lord and to meditate in His temple.

Psalm 63:6 When I remember You on my bed, I meditate on You in the night watches.

Psalm 77:6 I will remember my song in the night; I will meditate with my heart, and my spirit ponders:

Psalm 77:12 I will meditate on all Your work and muse on Your deeds.

Psalm 119:15 I will meditate on Your precepts and regard Your ways.

Psalm 119:23 Even though princes sit and talk against me, Your servant meditates on Your statutes.

Psalm 119:27 Make me understand the way of Your precepts, so I will meditate on Your wonders.

Psalm 119:48 And I shall lift up my hands to Your commandments, which I love; and I will meditate on Your statutes.

Psalm 119:78 ...But I shall meditate on Your precepts.

Psalm 119:148 My eyes anticipate the night watches, that I may meditate on Your word.

Psalm 143:5 I remember the days of old; I meditate on all Your doings; I muse on the word of Your hands.

Psalm 145:5 On the glorious splendor of Your majesty and on Your wonderful works, I will meditate.

Psalm 19:14 Let the words of my mouth and the meditation of my heart be acceptable in Your sight, O Lord, my rock and my Redeemer.

Psalm 49:3 My mouth will speak wisdom, and the meditation of my heart will be understanding.

Psalm 104:34 Let my meditation be pleasing to Him; as for me, I shall be glad in the Lord.

Psalm 119:97 O how I love Your law! It is my meditation all the day.

Psalm 119:99 I have more insight than all my teachers, for Your testimonies are my meditation.

■■

Don't be surprised if during your time of reflection, God shows you something. Our minds were created by a very creative God, so He often speaks to us through pictures; our imagination. In your own time, you might enjoy searching the scriptures regarding visions. Two particular verses in the book of Acts rock my mind regarding visions. I used to fear the words "visions" and "trance," but I realized it's Biblical. Some have misused these gifts from God, but we should not neglect such things just because they've been misused. In calling something good "evil," we deny ourselves an avenue of hearing the Holy Spirit and we deny a gift from our Father.

Peter reported in Acts 11:5, "I was in the city of Joppa praying; and in a trance I saw a vision..."

Paul reported in Acts 22:17, "It happened when I returned to Jerusalem and was praying in the temple, that I fell into a trance..."

You are in for a treat when you take time to focus on the Lord and who He is in you.

Father,

thank You
for Your goodness and mercy.

Thank You
for filling me with every good thing.

You are a beautiful Creator
And a majestic Author.

Come, Lord,
And fix my attention on You.

You are my Shepherd.

In You, I lack nothing.

I have no want.

I am fulfilled in You.

When I feel afraid,

When disappointment tries to convince
me that there is no escape from pain,

You gently remind me of what is true.

You speak to me
These words...

"The perfect peace above
is more true than the shadows
that surround you."

What is above is more true than what is
below.

Father,

You are perfect peace.

Perfect love casts out fear.

You are perfect love,
And I am in You.
You are in me.

Thank You for filling me

With Your perfect love
And the peace that passes understanding.

Above the storm,
calm skies always remain.

Jesus,
You taught that we are the salt of the earth
And the light of the world.
Because You have brought us
Into union with You,
We get to bring flavor and preservation to the earth.
We get to shine the light of hope to others.

You lead me beside still waters.
You light the way.
With You, I can sleep safely in the boat as
the storms of life rise against me.

Photo Credit: Traci Vanderbush

There is no reason to fear for my safety.
You sleep in the storm,
So I will, too.
I will lie down and rest with You.

After the storm passes,

You are always faithful to remind me of

the goodness ahead.

You promise to never leave me.

I am never alone in the storm.

Hope

And

Light

are sure to greet me

in the morning.

You restore my soul.

Again

And

Again,

You restore.

There will never be a time

When I am alone.

There will never be a moment

When I am abandoned.

I am held in the arms of

Perfect Love Himself.

There was never a time when I was
alone.

There was never a time when I was
abandoned.

You held me

When no one else would.

You loved me

When no one else did.

Your eyes of love looked upon me,

Absorbing my pain and disappointment.

You are good.

You are true.

**Even in the hard places,
I have life.**

Spirit,

In You there is no raging.

There is no doubt.

You give my eyes new vision to see

The goodness all around me.

I speak to my eyes,

"See in Him.

See as the Father sees.

Eyes,

You were made to see Him.

You were made to see others through

Him.

There is no more blindness.

My focus is on the Father,

The Son,

And the Holy Spirit.

Eyes, see clearly."

**The things of the past can no longer skew
my vision.
I will see as He sees.**

Father,

You bring everything into the light,

And I have no fear of those things.

I was made to walk with you upon the waters.

When the rains come again,

I remember not to be afraid.

The light of glory,

The hope-filled blue skies forever remain

shining above the darkness.

The waters restore.

The waters bring growth and life.

Soft clouds remind me of Your

gentleness.

You lead me in the paths of
righteousness.

You have set me right again,
On my feet once more.

I am no longer turned upside down by
the chaos that threatened me.

With You, I can never truly be
threatened.
You are at peace,
And so am I.
You walk with me, showing me what is
possible.

You satisfy my lips with goodness.

I speak to my body,

I speak to my soul,

BE WHOLE.

Every cell in my body, I call you good and
perfect.

Christ lives within you.
Every muscle and joint,

You are filled with
The goodness and power of God.

Yes, I am filled with the goodness and
power of God.
Even when I walk through the valleys and
the darkness that comes in this life,
I know that it is only a shadow.
Shadows have no power to harm me.
I am enveloped in Your embrace.

Your breath is within me.
What Your breath touches comes to life.
Mending happens.
I am re-membered, brought back
together into wholeness.

Your guidance and Your surety comfort me.
Who You are assures me.
You are always above all and in all,
Forever loving all that You have made.

A true artist, You are.
You breathed into every cell of my being
And infused me with Your own life and
blood.
My body is animated by You.
My soul is alive because of You.

My heart cannot remain locked

Behind doors of fear and hatred.

You held my heart in Your loving hands

Even in the midst of the noise.

When my soul was assaulted,

You did not abandon me.

You stood with me and wept with me,

But You refused to leave me locked in a

state of anxiety.

The Savior of my soul,

The One who rescues me

From my fears

And inspires me to dance in freedom.

You prepare for me a table of feasting.

Even in the presence of those who hate me,

You feed me the best that life has to offer.

You marked me for joy before I was ever born.
Every organ in my body is a recipient of the joy of Your heart.
I was made for joy.
Like the flowers in the field,
I will dance.
I surrender to the wind of Your Spirit.
I give myself to Your movement.

My body thrives in You, God.
Every tendon,
Ligament,
Muscle,
Organ,
And
Cell
Is saturated with Your presence.

My bones are filled with gratitude at the
reality of Your closeness.

You chose to make me Your temple.
How perfect is that place in which You
live.

When I think about what You have
created in this body,
I marvel over the miracle of life.

Your breath infuses me with energy and
makes me tall like the trees.

I breathe deeply and enjoy the freedom
of being whole in You.

I speak to the sadness stored inside of me
And I say to you, "Be filled with joy!
You were made for joy.

The trauma of the past has been drawn out of me.
The goodness of the Father is being poured into every facet, every crack and broken place within me.

Every bruise is being soothed by the loving hand of God as He embraces me.
All that died inside,
I call you to live again.

Rise and be whole.

Soul, be reformed.

Rise and be whole, my soul.

Body, the poison of pain and disappointment has been removed.
The knife of betrayal has been withdrawn.
The healing salve of Heaven is within you,
And you respond to its power.

**The coldness will turn to warmth.
The ice becomes water that gives life.**

Body,
I call every good memory
And every moment of joy
To the surface.
Every positive thing that has happened to you,
Every second of happiness,
And all of the love that has ever been given to you,
Be multiplied now.

Mind,
Recall every happy memory.
Remember everything that brought a smile.
Bring to the surface those things that brought life, love, joy and peace.

Soul,
Respond to every good thing.
Be saturated in the goodness of the Father as these gifts are remembered.

The joy is more true than the sadness.

Joy is eternal.

Sadness is momentary.

Each joyful memory is unique.

Like a snowflake,

A unique work of art

Specifically designed
and fashioned for me.

Each moment of joy
Is for me to meditate on
Until my body responds to that joy,
Embracing it as a legacy
To pass down to future generations.

Mind,
Remember them well.

Body,
Your ability to heal is greater than your
ability to become sick.

You are more susceptible to abundant life
than you are to illness.

You are more inclined to be healthy than
to be unwell.

You are more vulnerable to wholeness.

You are more receptive and responsive to
the goodness that exists in the earth.

You are wide open to blessing.

Now, lie down and rest in the bubbling
joy of the Father that rises up within you.

Every cell is being regenerated. They are
taking on a healthy form.

You are being filled with a spirit of hope
and joyful expectation.

Body, soul, spirit and mind,
This is what you were made for.
Laughter, joy, love, and purity.
This is your destiny.

You reflect all that is good and all that is right.

You look like your Father.

He lives in you and makes Himself known in you.

Rays of light and life come from you, affecting the world around you.

Through this love and goodness, others will come to know Him and shine as well.

Peace.

Be still.

Know that He is God.

You are in the Father,

He is in you,

And you are in Him.

John 14:20

Photo Credit: Traci Vanderbush

Goodness and light are never-ending.

Take a moment to reflect and write...

Our bodies and souls were created by a very creative Creator who delights in repair and restoration. What does this say about you and your purpose?

Think back as far as possible. What is the first happy moment you can recall?

Have you had an experience in which you felt "the fullness of joy?" If so, describe it here:

Find a photo of yourself as an infant, if possible. If you don't have one, try to envision yourself as a baby. Study your innocence. Take note of each detail: your little nose, fingers and toes. What expression do you see on your face? What would you imagine the destiny of that child to be?

What does the Father think of that baby? Before answering, take a moment to ask the Holy Spirit to show you something you've never seen. Write it here.

You are a dream of God's. Is that hard for you to believe? _____

He thought of you long before you were formed. Your soul was thriving in Him before He fashioned you with His hands and infused you with His breath. Can you imagine yourself in existence before you were born into this world?_____

If you could be born into this world once more, what would the ideal situation look like? What would life look like?

Do you believe that through God making all things new, you can still live the life you dreamed of?

Do you feel there are people holding you back from where you want to be? If so, feel free to list them here:

Will you allow these people to have power over you?_____Most likely, you answered, "no." Nobody wants to be overpowered, especially by those who have hurt them. If we do not choose forgiveness (releasing others from our judgments), we enslave ourselves to the wrongs they have done; we enslave ourselves to our own hatred and anger, allowing darkness to invade our hearts. This affects us on every level: body, soul, mind and spirit.

Close your eyes and ask the Holy Spirit to help you see your offender as an infant. What was their purpose and destiny? Ask Him to show you what may have gone wrong. What happened to them? How could it be made right? If you would like, write it here so that you don't forget:

Continue writing your thoughts on this page...

We have all been given free will, to do whatever we please. There are choices that produce life, and there are choices that cause pain and produce death. We have all chosen wrongly at times, and it's easy to forget the good that we have chosen. List some good choices you have made:

What good was produced from those choices you made?

As we walk through this journey of life, we must remember that what we know now is temporal. Though it be temporal, we are fully eternal, and what we know now is just the tiniest tip of the iceberg. When you think of eternity, how does it change your perspective of this life on earth?

Goodness and mercy follows you all the days of your life. And the Lord goes before you. If goodness follows you and your Father goes before you, everything you will ever face is surrounded by the promise of His presence. Was there a time when you believed He was nowhere to be found? Did you feel abandoned? If so, write about it here:

Ask the Holy Spirit to show you where He was at those moments. Where was your Father?

Hopefully, you saw that He was with you even in your darkest hours. Did you see His face? Did He weep with you? Spend some time thinking about this.

Everyone experiences negatives in their lifetime. In order to overcome those negatives, let's try to build bridges from them that lead to good thoughts. For example, "this bad thing happened, but it led to this good thing." This may be similar to a previous question, but I feel it's important to retrain our brains through repetition. List negatives that turned into positives:

Earlier in the book, I made this statement: "Some things we dreamed about are no longer an option for us, yet God has a beautifully incredible way of making that dream still come true, perhaps in another way or another form. Does this thought offend you? Is so, why?

Does that thought bring you hope? If so, think of a dream that died. How could God possibly make it come true at this point? Would it look different? Write your thoughts here:

There is still hope for dreams to come true on this earthly plane, and you can leave a legacy that will launch others into their dreams. In what ways do you feel capable of empowering others to see their dreams fulfilled?

There is scientific evidence that what is going on inside of us (in our hearts and minds) affects our bodies and everyone around us. List ten things that fill your heart with gratitude. Take time to focus on them daily.
1.
2.
3.
4.
5.
6.
7.
8.
9.
10.

Beloved, I pray that in all respects you may prosper and be in good health, just as your soul prospers.
3 John 1:2

Traci has created a variety of books for your enjoyment, from children's stories to life lessons, from fiction to non-fiction. Be sure to look for these works on Amazon.com or by visiting Tracivanderbush.wix.com/vanderbush

Walking With a Shepherd
The Magic of Our Forefathers
Vignette: Glimpses of Mysterious Love
The Porches of Holly
Mr. Thomas and the Cottonwood Tree
Life with Lummox
Lummox and the Happy Christmas
And more...

Made in the USA
Columbia, SC
04 April 2018